Let's Explore Rockport

By Zachary Malott

With help from daddy

Special thanks to
Grammy, David Robinson, Barbara and the office of the Cape Ann Chamber of
Commerce

©2017, Zachary Malott
All Rights Reserved
Published by the Malott Literary Group
Gloucester, MA
Email: litgroup@outlook.com

Welcome to the tip of Cape Ann and the small coastal village of Rockport. Rockport is an amazing place, it is very small and quaint, yet the whole day can quickly pass by because there is so much to do and see.

Before explorers and colonists stepped foot on Cape Ann, the area was home to the Native American Agawam tribe. Then in 1605, a French explorer named Samuel de Champlain named the peninsula; Cap Aux Isles after his expedition had landed here briefly. Champlain explorations were extensive including discoveries in the Caribbean,

Samuel de Champlain (1574-1635)

Florida, New Brunswick, and even was the first European explorer to travel and map the Great Lakes. From 1601 to 1603 Champlain served as a geographer in the court of King Henry IV. As part of his duties he traveled to French ports and learned much about North America from the fishermen that seasonally traveled to coastal areas from Nantucket to Newfoundland to capitalize on the rich fishing grounds there. Champlain's first trip to North America was as an observer on a fur-trading expedition led by François Gravé Du Pont.

DuPont was a navigator and merchant who had been a ship's captain on another expedition, and with whom Champlain established a firm lifelong friendship. He educated Champlain about navigation in North America, including the Saint Lawrence River, and in dealing with the natives there. In 1605 and 1606, Champlain explored the North American coast to establish settlements as far south as Cape Cod, searching for sites for a permanent settlement.

By the time the first Europeans founded a permanent settlement which was located in nearby Gloucester, the majority of the Agawam tribe had died from exposure to diseases they caught from the early contact with those Europeans. For over a hundred years Rockport was uninhabited and was used as a source for timber, primarily pine, which was used for building ships. Then in 1743 and with a thriving fishing industry around Cape Ann a dock was constructed at Rockport Harbor on Sandy Bay which was used to load and ship timber and fish.

By the start of the 19th century, granite quarries were producing massive amounts of granite which was being shipped throughout the East Coast.

photo-Cape Ann Museum

Men working in the granite quarries in Rockport

Granite was harvested from quarries dug deep in the earth creating a thriving business on Cape Ann from the 1830s through the early 20th century, second only to fishing in economic output. For 100 years the granite trade played a huge role in the local economy providing jobs for people from throughout New England and around the world.

Construction of a fort in Boston Harbor in 1798 followed by a jail in nearby Salem in 1813, jump started the granite business on Cape Ann. During the 1830s and 1840s, the trade grew steadily. By the 1850s, the stone business was well established and Cape Ann granite was known throughout the region. So extensive were operations during the second half of the 19th century that some feared the business might actually run out of stone.

Loading granite at the Granite Pier in Rockport

Blocks were packed aboard specially designed sloops and transported to distant ports.

Cut granite stones

Tons upon tons of paving stones were shipped out of Cape Ann, destined for construction projects in New York, Boston, and Philadelphia and all along the Atlantic seaboard.

During Rockport's early days Rockport was primarily made up of large estates, summer homes and a small fishing village during a time that most people were living in nearby Gloucester. In 1840, Rockport became its own town and was incorporated because its small number of residents wanted an identity of its own. The large majority of Rockport's citizens were of Scandinavian descent.

During the period of the "Great Depression" the granite industry greatly declined but Rockport still thrived as an artist's colony. Known for its popularity as a vacation destination because of its rocky, boulder-strewn beaches, its history as a great fishing harbor and its popularity from Rudyard Kipling's book; Captains Courageous.

Turks Head Inn, circa. 1910

The present day community of Rockport is small and very close. Most people in Rockport know each other and the vibe here is one which is very outgoing and welcoming.

Homes in present day Rockport The neighborhoods around Rockport have a laid back, New England, beach feel to them.

Unquestionably Rockport's number one recognized point of interest is Motif #1 which is located on Bradley Wharf and is a replica of a former fishing shack well known to students of art and art history as "the most often-painted building in America." During the 1840s as Rockport was becoming home to a colony of artists and settlement of fishermen, the shack became a favorite subject of painters due to the composition and lighting of its location as well as being a symbol of New England maritime life.

The original structure was built in 1840 but it was destroyed in the Blizzard of 1978. An exact replica was reconstructed that same year. Motif No. 1 was first used for storing gear and fish. It is so iconic that it has even been featured on a postage stamp.

Artists painting Motif #1 circa 1960

Painter Lester Hornby (1882–1956) is believed to be the first to call the shack "Motif Number 1," a reference to its being the favorite subject of the town's painters, and the name achieved general acceptance.

In the 1930s, painter John Buckley used the shack as his studio. He sold it to the town in 1945, dedicated "In 1945, the town of Rockport purchased the Motif as a monument to Rockport residents who had served in the Armed Services."

Rockport locals, recognizing its iconic value, have taken steps to preserve both its structure and appearance, finding a red paint which appears weather-beaten even when new, and keeping the area clear of overhead wires, traffic signs and advertising.

In 1933, the Rockport Legionnaires decided to build a replica float of the Motif for the American Legion's convention in Chicago, which coincided with the World's Fair. The float was driven to Chicago over three days on an old bus chassis. At night it stopped, illuminated by floodlights, and brochures about Rockport were distributed to passersby. In Chicago, the float was parked at Navy Pier where thousands came to take pictures of it.

On April 4, 2002, Motif No. 1 graced a postage stamp as part of the postal service's "Greetings from America."

Just about every part of Rockport offers a view of Motif #1. When the sun is setting is a time to get some great photos.

For more than the past 60 years, Rockport has held a festival called 'Motif # 1 Day. There's even a Motif #1 Short Film Festival in Rockport.

The original Motif #1 was destroyed by a blizzard in 1978.

The downtown area is a major tourist destination and attracts millions of visitors annually, mostly during the summer months.

Most everything in centrally located around the downtown area.

The downtown village area is filled with very colorful stores and everything seems to have a nautical theme to its character.

In the downtown area you'll find art galleries and rows of gift and souvenir shops that line the streets.

Keep an eye out for the Happy Whale, its Rockport's toy store and is packed with lots of very awesome toys!

The downtown area is really an exciting place to explore and very much fits what you'd expect from a New England coastal fishing village. That is part of its charm that attracts so many visitors to the area daily.

Bearskin Neck Jetty is right downtown at the end of Bearskin Neck. I don't, but some people like to walk out a ways on the jetty for a good location to take pictures. There is no paved walkway so people have to step from rock to rock. It's too scary for me.

The Roy Moore Lobster Company is a New England legend for fresh sea food and is located on Bearskin Neck. You can't miss their trademark big red lobster sign in front. It has been said by many that here you will get the best lobster roll in all New England.

Front Beach

Right on the edge of town is Front Beach. It is very accessible from downtown if you wanted to take a break from shopping and stick your toes into some warm, soft sand and relax for a bit.

Long Beach

Long Beach is off Thatcher Road and is another stretch of ocean and sand, backed by a cement retaining wall and lined with summer cottages. There are great views here of Thatcher's Island and the lighthouses. There is also a Rockport end and a Gloucester end to this stretch of beach.

Cape Hedge Beach

If you are looking for a more quiet and secluded Beach, Cape Hedge Beach may be just what you're looking for. Unless you're a resident you'll need a seasonal sticker, and parking here is very limited. However, this is a beautiful beach, not found by many people. The beach is down Route 127a and you turn right at the Turk's Head Inn.

Pebble Beach

Pebble Beach gets its name from, you guessed it! It's pebble beach. But the pebbles are smooth and rounded because of the constant tidal motion. The beach is located at the end of South Street.

Old Garden Beach

Old Garden Beach is also accessible by a short walk from downtown. It's a small sand and stone beach with an adjacent municipal park and has a beautiful view over Sandy Bay and also has areas for picnics.

Back Beach

Back Beach is also close to downtown and offers soft sand and great views. This is more of an explorer's beach than a swimming beach and is renowned for scuba diving.

The view of Rockport Harbor from the Headlands.

This is a great place to get amazing views of downtown Rockport, the harbor, and Motif #1 and just a short walk from downtown.

The locals know all the good swimming spots around the local quarries in Rockport. They are popular swimming holes with crystal clear water and cliffs to jump from.

The Rockport Granite Company, which operated from 1865 to 1933, built this 65-foot arched bridge in 1872.

It was one of the largest bridges at the time and supported the main highway between Rockport and Pigeon Cove and still stands strong today though long abandoned.

Without question the Shalin Liu Performance Center is an amazing live music venue located in downtown Rockport.

The place is small and intimate and actually puts on many shows by major stars who look forward to performing here. The Center also boosts an excellent classical music line up. The backdrop of the stage features a huge window looking out over the ocean. It is a spectacular and very beautiful theatre.

Ok guy's that pretty much sums it up for the best things to see and do in Rockport. I hope you had fun reading about Rockport and I hope you get a chance to visit this amazing place. I always have a great time when I go and often discover new places and things to do. You may discover something I haven't yet that's not in my book.

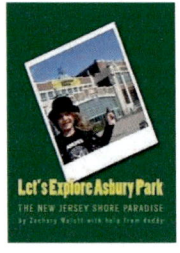    

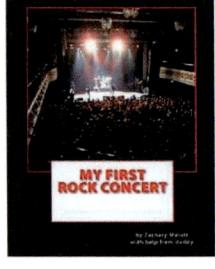

Made in the USA
Middletown, DE
02 February 2019